FERRARI

A celebration of an iconic marque

Mason Crest

Contents

Mason Crest
450 Parkway Drive, Suite D
Broomall, PA 19008
www.masoncrest.com

©2016 by Mason Crest, an imprint of National Highlights, Inc.

Printed and bound in the United States of America.

10 9 8 7 6 5 4 3 2

Cataloging-in-Publication Data on file with the Library of Congress.

Series ISBN: 978-1-4222-3275-0
Hardback ISBN: 978-1-4222-3279-8
ebook ISBN: 978-1-4222-8517-6

Written by: Jed Paine

Images courtesy of Magic Car Pics, Corbis and Shutterstock

Introduction

In 1898, a boy who was destined to achieve great things was born in the Italian city of Modena. Enzo Ferrari would go on to be renowned for being the founder of the world-class sports car manufacturer in both racing and road categories. Ferraris are best known for their sleek, stunning, curvaceous design, eye-watering price tag, and standard rosso corsa (race red) paintwork. From the very first Ferrari, the 1947 Tipo 125 S racing sports car, through to the most recent 2013 LaFerrari mild hybrid limited edition road car, Ferrari have continued to astound enthusiasts and critics alike with their evolutionary performance road vehicles and Formula 1 racing pedigree.

During his youth, Enzo Ferrari dreamed of becoming a world-class racing driver and set out to pursue his dream. In 1920, Alfa Romeo spotted the young driver and recruited Ferrari as a test driver, where he later formed his own team, Scuderia Ferrari, to prepare and race the Alfa Romeos. Ferrari started manufacturing his own branded automobiles at the end of World War II, and it was from here that the legend of Ferrari flourished.

Ferrari have since gone on to become the most identifiable sports car manufacturer in history.

■ **BELOW: Enzo Ferrari.**

Foundation and History

The Ferrari journey began when the young Enzo Ferrari made his competitive debut in the Parma Poggio di Berceto hillclimb race in 1919. Driving a 2.3L four-cylinder CMN 15/20, the 21-year-old came fourth. Of the 47 races he entered, he won only 13, and in the mid-1920s he decided to pursue his love of building racing cars. In 1929 he formed Scuderia Ferrari in Modena with the aim of concentrating solely on motorsports; his racing "stable" (translating from scuderia) would offer amateur owner-drivers the opportunity to race. The company had no initial desire to produce road cars and its early years remained utterly focused on the manufacture of racing cars and sponsoring

drivers. Enzo Ferrari decided to quit competitive racing with the approaching birth of his son Alfredo (better known as Dino) and his ever-growing workload as the head of Scuderia. His final race was behind the wheel of an Alfa Romeo 8C 2300MM at the Circuito Tre Province on August 9, 1931, where he finished in second place.

Ferrari enjoyed success preparing cars and racing drivers (often in Alfa Romeos) and by 1933 he had taken over Alfa Romeo's racing department. In 1937 Scuderia Ferrari built the Alfa Romeo 158 Alfetta: it would become one of the most successful racing cars ever produced, winning 47 of the 54 Grands Prix that it was entered in.

■ **LEFT:** The sleek red lines of the Ferrari: a world record 964 Ferraris parade around the Silverstone F1 circuit.

■ **BELOW:** Enzo Ferrari testing his eight-cylinder Alfa Romeo, 1924.

■ **ABOVE:** A side view of the Auto Avio Costruzioni 815 (AAC 815), which was driven by Alberto Ascari in the 1940 Mille Miglia. This car is in the Mario Righini Collection at Panzano Castle in Italy.

■ **RIGHT:** The Ferrari factory in Modena, Italy.

Upon his departure from Alfa Romeo in 1938, Enzo Ferrari was prohibited from using the Ferrari name in association with racing cars for four years, so he formed Auto Avio Costruzioni (AAC) to produce machine tools and aircraft accessories. In December 1939, Lotario Rangoni, Marquis di Modena, commissioned Enzo to build two racing cars for him and fellow racing driver Alberto Ascari to drive in the 1940 Brescia Grand Prix. Named the Tipo 815, this was Ferrari's first car, but due to the impact of World War II it saw little competition.

The Ferrari factory moved to Maranello in 1943 and has remained there to this day. The factory was bombed in 1944 and it was not until the war ended that the factory was rebuilt to include a road car production facility in 1946.

The first car to bear the Ferrari name was the 125 S (commonly known as the 125 or 125 Sport): a racing sports car that made its

world debut at the Piacenza Racing Circuit in 1947. A 1.5L V12 engine powered the 125 S, an ambitious feat of engineering in this era. It was with reluctance that Enzo Ferrari built and sold these cars, but funding Scuderia Ferrari was his priority.

In 1949, Ferrari made their first major move into the grand touring market with the launch of the 166 Inter, setting a high standard of both style and engineering. This was an important development in Ferrari history: to this day the bulk of their sales derive from the grand touring market. In 1951 a significant relationship between Ferrari and Carrozzeria Pininfarina (formerly Pinin Farina) was established through the body styling of the 212 Inter. Pininfarina have since designed all but two road-going production cars: the 1973 Dino 308 GT4 and 2013's LaFerrari. The relationship between Pininfarina and Ferrari was so solid that they became partners in Scuderia Ferrari

■ ABOVE: A 1947 Ferrari 125 S at Galleria Ferrari in Maranello, Italy.

SpA SEFAC (Scuderia Enzo Ferrari Auto Corse), the organization behind the Ferrari racing team between 1961 and 1989.

Carrozzeria Scaglietti, another noteworthy coachbuilder, designed a number of Ferrari models throughout the late 1950s and throughout the 1960s. Only exclusively designed Scaglietti models, such as the Ferrari 250 Testa Rossa, carried their badge. Several desired models among collectors include the 250 California, 250 GTO, and 250 Tour de France – Scaglietti built these to a Pininfarina design.

In 1956, Enzo Ferrari was left devastated after his son Dino died of muscular dystrophy. Before his death, Dino had been contributing ideas to the production of a new 1500 cc V6 engine during discussions with his father and engineer Vittorio Jano. When the engine debuted 10 months after his death Ferrari announced that the V6-engined series of race and road cars would be named in his honor.

The Dino brand was created to market affordable sports cars that would not diminish the Ferrari mystique. These were the first mid-engined Ferraris and, although this was common in the world

of sports car racing, the layout in a production car was daring for its time.

It became evident that in order for the company to continue to develop they would need to find a powerful partner, leading to the Fiat Group taking a 50 per cent stake in Ferrari. This investment allowed for a factory extension, and production of the Ferrari-engineered Fiat Dino was transferred from Fiat's Turin plant.

The last model to be personally approved by Enzo Ferrari was the

■ ABOVE: A publicity shot of the Fiat Dino Spider.

F40, a car that many believe is the "greatest supercar the world has ever seen." The 40th-anniversary model was the fastest and most powerful car built by Ferrari to be sold to the public at the time. It went on sale with a suggested retail price of $400,000, although high demand for the car led to sales topping $1.6 million.

All Ferraris bear the instantly identifiable badge of the rearing black stallion on a yellow shield with the letters S F, and three stripes in reference to the Italian national colors. This iconic symbol, cavallino rampante (prancing horse), brands every Ferrari and can be traced back to the company's early years. On June 17, 1923, Enzo Ferrari was victorious in his race in the Circuito del Savio at Ravenna where he met Countess Paolina, the mother of World War I hero Francesco Baracca. Baracca would paint a prancing red horse on a white background on the side of his planes, and the Countess asked Enzo to do the same, suggesting that it would bring him good luck. Ferrari agreed and chose to have the horse painted in black. The canary yellow background on which it stands is the color of the city of Modena, Enzo's birthplace.

Since the 1920s, Ferrari have used rosso corsa as the key color of their cars. This was the national racing color of Italy, as recommended by what was later to become the FIA (Fédération Internationale de l'Automobile). Colors related to nationality rather than car manufacturer or driver, so Italian race cars including Ferrari, Alfa Romeo, and Maserati would be painted red, whereas French-based manufacturer Bugatti used blue, German-based manufacturer Mercedez used white, and British-based manufacturer Lotus used green.

In 2008, Fiat increased its stake in Ferrari and now owns 85 per cent of the company; Enzo's second son, Piero Ferrari, owns 10 per cent, and the remaining five per cent belongs to the Mubadala Development Company.

■ **ABOVE: The black stallion on a yellow shield is instantly recognizable as the Ferrari brand.**

■ **RIGHT: Piero Ferrari owns a minority shareholding in Ferrari, retaining the family's involvement in the company.**

166 Inter/195 Inter

Powered by a narrow-angle 60° V12 engine, the 166 Inter set a high standard of style and engineering as Ferrari's first road car. This elegant coupe was designed by Carrozzeria Touring of Milan, a renowned design house that had previously worked on numerous Alfa Romeo models. The 166 Inter's style was reminiscent of the 166 MM Barchetta, but with the addition of a smoothly curved coupe body. The chassis, although designed by Ferrari, was produced by specialized Gilco in Italy and was lengthened to 95.3 in (2420 mm), supporting the Gioacchino Colombo-designed V12

engine and five-speed transmission, comparable to the 166 MM competition car. Ferrari produced around 20 hand-built 166s, allowing clients to indulge in personal styling and preference so that each car was unique.

Produced by Ferrari in 1950, and introduced at the Paris Motor Show of the same year, the 195 Inter shared many design features with the 166 Inter, however the wheelbase had been stretched by 3.1 in (80 mm) to 98.4 in (2500 mm) and the V12 engine increased to 2341 cc, enabling it to deliver 130 bhp and a top speed of 120 mph.

Produced	1948-1950 (166 Inter)/ 1950 (195 Inter)
Engine Size	1995 cc
Cylinders	12
0-60 mph	11.1 secs
Top Speed	106 mph
Power Output	109 bhp
Transmission	Manual
Gears	5 Speed
Length	156.7 in (3980 mm)
Width	60 in (1525 mm)
Height	53.1 in (1350 mm)
Weight	1984 lb (900 kg)
Wheelbase	95.3 in 2420 mm

(Specifications refer to the 166 Inter)

212 Inter

After the previous success of the 166 and 195 Inters, Ferrari developed the 212 Inter in 1951 and unveiled it later that year at the Brussels Motor Show. Evolving from the design of the 166, the 212 gained a reputation for being a sports car for the road that could also win international races. The bored-out V12 engine achieved a 2562 cc displacement. While only one Weber carburetor was used, it packed a punch of 130 bhp with a top speed of 120 mph. Export versions featured three Weber carburetors, producing 150 bhp and a top speed of 140 mph.

Around 110 cars were made, each having been specially ordered by clients with personal styling and mechanical specification taken into account. While some cars received competition-spec upgrades, others sported luxurious interiors and finely decorated bodies. Each car was unique; it is the individuality of these cars that makes the 212 Inter series so interesting. Coachbuilders that worked on the bodies included Carrozzeria Touring, Vignale, Ghia, and Pininfarina. The relationship established with Pininfarina during the production of the 212 was an important development for Ferrari and still exists today.

Produced	1951-1952
Engine Size	2562 cc
Cylinders	12
0-60 mph	10.5 secs
Top Speed	120 mph
Power Output	130 bhp
Transmission	Manual
Gears	5 Speed
Length	161.4 in (4100 mm)
Width	60 in (1525 mm)
Height	51 in (1295 mm)
Weight	2425 lb (1100 kg)
Wheelbase	102.4 in (2600 mm)

(Specifications refer to the 212 Inter base model)

250

During the early 1950s, Ferrari manufactured one of their most popular vehicle lines: the 250 series. First introduced at the 1953 Paris Motor Show, the Europa was one of the earlier 250 series to be seen by the public. Heralded as the vehicle that had taken over from its predecessor, the 212 Inter, the 250 Europa was built around the chassis of a 375 America and bore some similarities in aesthetics. The front-engined Europa was generously powered by a 3L Lampredi V12, kicking out a surprising 200 bhp and a top speed of 135 mph, 11 mph faster than the 212 Inter. Initial lines

Produced	1953-1964
Engine Size	2963 cc
Cylinders	12
0-60 mph	5.9 secs
Top Speed	135 mph
Power Output	200 bhp
Transmission	Manual
Gears	4 Speed
Length	110.2 in (2800 mm)
Width	52.2 in (1325 mm)
Height	51.9 in (1320 mm)
Weight	2359 lb (1070 kg)
Wheelbase	110.2 in (2800 mm)

(Specifications refer to the 250 Europa)

of the Europa, bodied by Vignale, had visual similarities to the 340 Mexico until production was taken over by Pininfarina, who went on to produce a two-seater cabriolet version alongside the original model. Within a year of its debut, the Europa was swiftly replaced with the 250 Europa GT that featured some modifications and was designed to entirely replace the original model. For a short while the GT was still referred to purely as the 250 Europa, but the Europa suffix was to be dropped entirely further down the line, leaving the car to be known henceforth as simply the 250 GT.

The latter form of the Europa (250 GT) had its engine replaced with a Colombo short block V12, allowing for a variety of modifications to be made, enhancing the performance of the car. Among the changes were

the reduction of the wheelbase by 7.87 in (down to 102.4 in [2600 mm]), while the front and rear tracks were increased by 1.14 in (29 mm). The 250 Europa GT was constructed around longitudinal steel tubes with cross bracing and outriggers for support. The main chassis tubes were positioned above the rear axle rather than under it, as previously positioned on the 250 Europa and 375 America models. In terms of making Ferrari history, the 250 series marked the pinnacle point where Pininfarina took over as the sole production company of Ferrari production cars. The 250s were manufactured between 1953 and 1964; they were finally taken off the production line to make way for the Ferrari 275 GTB.

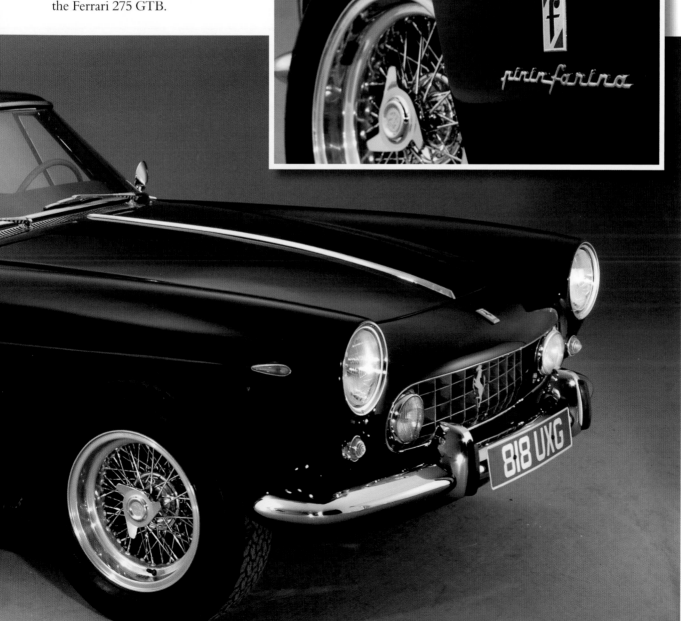

250 GTO

Of all the Ferraris to date, the 250 GTO has received the most acclaim. It was unlike many other Ferraris because it was not designed by a specific design house or individual: Giotto Bizzarrini was the chief engineer and he worked alongside Sergio Scaglietti, who developed the body, perfecting its design through wind tunnel and on-track testing. By installing the 3.0L V12 engine of the 250 GT SWB into the chassis of the 250 Testa Rossa, Ferrari had developed the 250 GTO: the ultimate car designed for GT racing that boasted both performance and styling. The shape of the aluminum body changed very little during production, with the exception of a one-off example sporting 330 LM Berlinetta styling. The final three cars of the series received a Pininfarina and Scaglietti collaborated body similar to the 250 LM sports racing car.

According to FIA regulations, a minimum of 100 examples of the car had to be built in order for it to be approved for Group 3 Grand Touring Car racing, however only 39 cars were ever produced. To bypass the regulations, Ferrari numbered the chassis at random. This out-of-sequence numbering gave the illusion that more cars had been produced. The 250 GTO made its racing debut at 12 Hours of Sebring and finished in second place. It went on to win the over 2000 cc class of the FIA's International Championship for GT Manufacturers in 1962, 1963, and 1964, and was one of the last front-engined cars to remain competitive at the top level of sports car racing. This dual-purpose car was at ease on the track and on the road, and only an elite selection of the

Produced	1962-1964
Engine Size	2953 cc
Cylinders	12
0-60 mph	5.4 secs
Top Speed	174 mph
Power Output	302 bhp
Transmission	Manual
Gears	5 Speed
Length	170. 3 in (4325 mm)
Width	63 in (1600 mm)
Height	47.6 in (1210 mm)
Weight	1940 lb (880 kg) dry
Wheelbase	94.5 in (2400 mm)

(Specifications refer to the 250 GTO base model)

motoring fraternity was fortunate enough to own one. Buyers had to be personally approved by both Enzo Ferrari and his dealer for North America, Luigi Chinetti.

In 2004 the 250 GTO was nominated as "top sports car of all time" by *Sports Car International* and it was placed in eighth position on the list of "top sports cars of the 1960s," while *Motor Trend Classic* gave the 250 GTO pole position on the list of the "greatest Ferraris of all time."

330

Ferrari introduced the 330 series in 1963 with the 330 America, built on the same chassis used for the 250 GTE. The America was swiftly replaced with the updated 330 GT 2+2, which featured a different engine configuration and twin-mounted headlights on the front end. The 330 GT 2+2 featured the Tipo 209 unit: a 4L front-mounted 60° V12 which delivered 300 bhp, enabling 0-60 in a surprising 6.3 seconds and a maximum speed of 152 mph. The GT 2+2 replaced the 330 America in January 1964 and was unveiled to the public at the Brussels Show. Standard equipment included Borrani wire wheels and a five-speed gearbox, replacing the four-speed transmission found in earlier models. Pininfarina was again behind the design and construction of the vehicle; they made two versions of the car that differed only in the design of the front end and the gearbox configuration: the earlier version (from 1963-1965) had four headlamps, whereas the later version (1965-1967) featured just the two.

Among other design upgrades, the 330 GT featured a dual-circuit Dunlop braking system, considered slightly unique in the way that it separated the brakes as front and rear rather than the common diagonal braking system that was found on modern cars. Pininfarina designed the car with smoother lines and a sleeker aesthetic than its predecessor; with its generous rounded tail end it provided the vehicle with a larger boot space. Constructed around the common Ferrari steel tubular chassis with extensive supportive cross bracing, the 330 GT 2+2 featured independent front suspension and a rigid rear axle that used microscopic shock absorbers. In the later years of the 330, power assisted steering and air conditioning became available as optional extras, while both left- and right-hand drives were commonly available. Production of the 330 GT 2+2 was halted in 1967 when the 365 GT 2+2 took the position of its predecessor. During its production, Pininfarina produced 1,099 of the 330 GT 2+2 (consisting of both series 1 and 2 cars), demonstrating that the series was indeed in good demand for its time.

Produced	1963-1967
Engine Size	3967 cc
Cylinders	12
0-60 mph	6.3 secs
Top Speed	152 mph
Power Output	300 bhp
Transmission	Manual
Gears	5 Speed
Length	190.5 in (4840 mm)
Width	67.5 in (1715 mm)
Height	53.5 in (1360 mm)
Weight	3042 lb (1380 kg)
Wheelbase	104.3 in (2650 mm)

(Specifications refer to the 330 GT 2+2)

275

Although not the first of the 275
production line, the 275 GT
Berlinetta was a strong contender
in the 275 series. Introduced at the
1964 Paris Salon, the Pininfarina-
designed, Scaglietti-constructed
275 GTB was heralded for two
major landmarks in Ferrari road
car production history. Firstly, the
275 GTB featured a differential
unit in conjunction with a
combined gearbox with a transaxle
assembly and, secondly, it had an
independent rear suspension. This
impressive new design boasted a
front-engined Colombo 60° 3.2L
V12 that punched a surprising
160 mph and 280 bhp. The long
and smooth lines that Pininfarina
had designed allowed for the
discretionary concealment of the
inner mechanical elements, such as
headlamp wiring.

In 1965, just one year after being
unveiled to the world of motoring,
the car received an upgrade in the
type 2 series, where it was given
a longer nose and flatter front
end, alongside the increased rear
windscreen size and larger boot
capacity. The chassis design of the
275 GTB series featured a tapering
rear tube element in order to house
the redesigned rear suspension and
transmission assembly. The initial
series of the 275 was constructed
on a tubular steel chassis frame,
with an aluminum bonnet, boot lid,
and doors, however, the later series
encompassed an entirely aluminum
covering. Around 450 examples of
the 275 GTB were manufactured
before production ceased in 1968,
when the car had been surpassed by
its successor the 365 GTB/4, more
commonly known as the Daytona.

Produced	1964-1968
Engine Size	3286 cc
Cylinders	12
0-60 mph	6.6 secs
Top Speed	160 mph
Power Output	280 bhp
Transmission	Manual
Gears	5 Speed
Length	170.3 in (4325 mm)
Width	67.9 in (1725 mm)
Height	49 in (1245 mm)
Weight	2425 lb (1100 kg)
Wheelbase	94.5 in (2400 mm)

(Specifications refer to the 275 GT Berlinetta)

MCH 951D

365

Unveiled during the 1966 Geneva Motor Show, the Ferrari 365 California set the benchmark for luxurious high-performance sports cars. This Pininfarina-designed convertible was manufactured with the intention of replacing its predecessor: the 500 Superfast. Whilst the 365 California's chassis was structurally identical in shape to the Superfast, the bodywork was given a cabriolet look and fast became the ultimate open top Italian sports car. The 365 California was not, however, an affordable vehicle: the very high retail price only attracted the elite top end of the automotive market and only 14 were ever built. The high-performance sports car was a front-engined, longitudinal positioned 60° 4.4L V12 that boasted an incredible 320 bhp and a top speed of 152 mph, highly competitive against other cars of

this caliber during the 1960s.

As with the earlier Superfast, the California type 598 chassis were sent to the Pininfarina factory in Grugliasco, where they were bodied and trimmed then returned to Ferrari for the fitting of the mechanical components

and detailing. The door design of the California featured a scalloped arrowhead shape near the upper edge with a chrome trim running through the center, which incorporated the door handle; this was a Pininfarina design feature that had previously been seen

on a Dino prototype introduced in 1965. Other notable features of the California were situated within the interior of the car. Electric windows were fitted as standard and the rev counter and speedometer were encompassed in large circular pods directly in front of the driver. The California design saw the disappearance of exterior release handles for the boot lid and fuel access flap; they were replaced by a pair of chrome-plated levers on the inside rear cabin trim panel. While heralded as the 1960s' most luxurious sports car, the California was swiftly replaced by the more popular 365 GT 2+2 in 1968, which went on to sell over 800 units. In June 2005 a pristinely kept California sold for a staggering $890,000.

Produced	1966-1970
Engine Size	4390 cc
Cylinders	12
0-60 mph	7.1 secs
Top Speed	152 mph
Power Output	320 bhp
Transmission	Manual
Gears	5 Speed
Length	192.9 in (4900 mm)
Width	70 in (1780 mm)
Height	52.4 in (1330 mm)
Weight	2910 lb (1320 kg)
Wheelbase	104.3 in (2650 mm)

(Specifications refer to the 365 California)

365 Daytona

The Ferrari 365 GTB/4, better known by its unofficial name the 365 Daytona, made its debut at the Paris Motor Show in 1968. The name was first given by the media in reference to Ferrari's 1-2-3 finish at the 24 Hours of Daytona, with their prototype sports car the 330P4. The 365 Daytona featured a traditional front engine and rear-wheel drive.

The Tipo 251 engine was developed from the earlier Columbia V12 used in its predecessor, the 275 GTB/4, and could produce 352 bhp, enabling 0-60 in 5.4 seconds and a top speed of 174 mph. The chassis, suspension, wheelbase, and even the layout, were very reminiscent of the former Berlinetta. The five-speed manual transmission was mounted in the rear for optimal weight distribution.

The 365 Daytona was designed by Leonardo Fioravanti at Pininfarina. Its sharp-edged appearance was unlike previous Ferrari models and it resembled a design familiar with Lamborghini. Early models featured fixed headlamps, but changes in safety regulations led to the Daytona sporting the pop-up variety that became customary for many models.

In its heyday it was the fastest-going road car and set a benchmark among supercar manufacturers. The car was voted "top sports car of the 1970s" by *Sports Car International* magazine in 2004, and *Motor Trend Classic* hailed the 365 GTB/4 into second position on the list of "greatest Ferraris of all time."

In addition to the Berlinetta, Ferrari (with Scaglietti) produced a limited run of Spiders –

the result was the 354 GTS. Although virtually identical to their Berlinetta counterparts, the body, chassis, and windshield frame were strengthened to convertible standard. With only 122 produced it is not surprising that they became very sought after models, and many Berlinettas have since been modified into convertibles. However, the varying

Produced	1968-1976
Engine Size	4390 cc
Cylinders	12
0-60 mph	5.4 secs
Top Speed	174 mph
Power Output	352 bhp
Transmission	Manual
Gears	5 Speed
Length	174.2 in (4425 mm)
Width	69.3 in (1760 mm)
Height	49 in (1245 mm)
Weight	2645 lb (1200 kg)
Wheelbase	94.5 in (2400 mm)

(Specifications refer to the 365 Daytona base model)

levels of quality achieved by these modifications have simply boosted the desire among Ferrari collectors for the original Scaglietti Spiders.

In 1969 Ferrari produced a competition version of the 365 GTB/4. The aluminum-bodied car was entered into Le Mans 24 Hour Race, although it crashed during practice. It was not until 1970 that Ferrari produced further racing versions of the 365 GTB/4.

Dino

Designed by Pininfarina, the 206 GT was first assembled in 1968 as a direct competitor for Porsche's 911. Dino was a brand in itself (shared by Fiat and Ferrari) and was named after Enzo Ferrari's late son Alfredo Dino Ferrari after his passing in 1956; the cars were manufactured with a Dino name badge and not branded as Ferraris until 1976. Although the Dino series was more extensive than just this one model (also featuring the Dino 246 GT, Dino 246 GTS, and Dino 306 GT4), it was the 206 GT that was marketed as an "affordable sports car," causing controversy among critics and Ferrari enthusiasts; the original marketing materials even suggested that the Dino 206 was "almost a Ferrari." Ferrari produced this budget road-going vehicle with the intention of boosting sales while also cutting production costs. The Dino 206 GT was the first Ferrari in the company's history that could

Produced	1968-1976
Engine Size	1987 cc
Cylinders	6
0-60 mph	7.5 secs
Top Speed	146 mph
Power Output	180 bhp
Transmission	Manual
Gears	5 Speed
Length	163.4 in (4150 mm)
Width	66.9 in (1700 mm)
Height	43.9 in (1115 mm)
Weight	1984 lb (900 kg)
Wheelbase	89.8 in (2280 mm)

(Specifications refer to the Dino 206 GT)

be assembled on a production line. Because of a recent change in Formula 2's monoposto legislation regarding the production of engines put into sports vehicles, Ferrari made the brave move to team up with Fiat, who began producing their engines to keep production costs down. It wasn't until the enthusiasts got behind the wheel for the first time that they realized the true credibility of the Dino 206 GT.

Making its debut at the 1965 Paris Motor Show, the 206 GT was hailed as a road-sturdy vehicle that featured the looks of a racing car. The 2L mid-engine sports car had demonstrated a top speed of 146 mph from its 65° V6, kicking out an impressive 180 bhp – much more than critics had expected from this affordable sports model. The 206 GT had a torque of 138 pounds per foot (at 6500 rpm) and was the first Ferrari model to ever feature a direct rack and pinion steering system. Another unique quality of the 206 GT was the fact that it was the first Ferrari to utilize an electronic ignition system (the Dinoplex C, capacitive discharge ignition system as designed by Magneti Marelli). The Ferrari Dino 206 GTs were produced over a one-year period (between 1968 and 1969) and only 152 were built before slight modifications were made in subsequent variants.

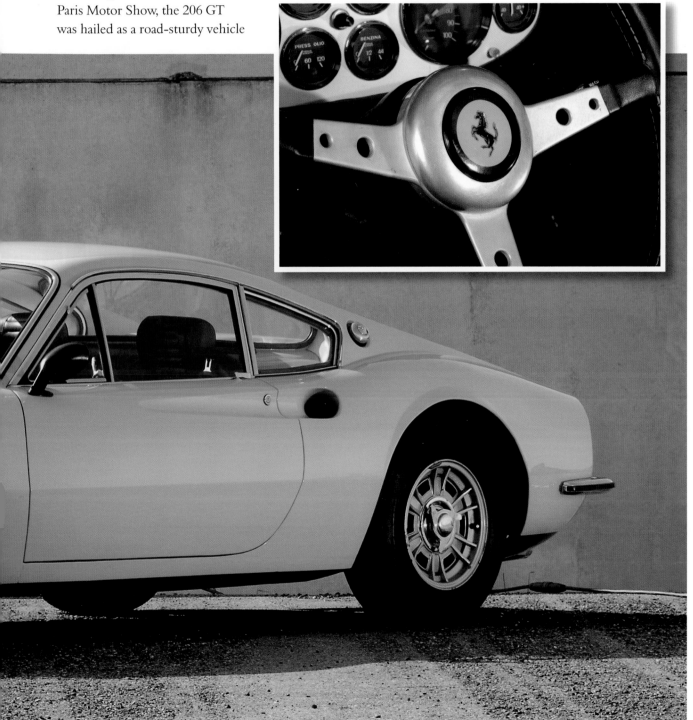

Berlinetta Boxer

First unveiled in 1971 at the Turin Motor Show (although not put into production until 1973), the 365 GT4 BB explored new territories: it was one of the first Ferrari top performance vehicles to feature a mid-positioned engine. Designed by Leonardo Fioravanti at Pininfarina, the 365 GT4 BB had two distinctive new features that set it aside from its direct competitors: the 12-cylinder engine derived from the Formula 1 car and the newly explored position of the engine that had not been seen before in a road car. The majority of its predecessors had featured the front-positioned engine, while the all-new 365 boasted a mid-position; it had taken the designers some time to convince Enzo Ferrari to adopt the idea. Closely matched in many ways to the Daytona, the 365 had a slightly higher horsepower of 360 bhp and a longitudinally mounted engine at 180°, as in their 1970 Formula 1 car. The 4.3L V12 and slender, yet aggressive, body shape meant that the 365 could reach a top speed of 186 mph and 0-60 in 5.4 seconds. The contoured body design of the 365 featured a reshaped front end that was based on the Pininfarina P6 concept car, originally unveiled at the 1968 Turin Motor Show.

Pininfarina designed the car with a recess under the front lid in which a spare "space-saving" tire was concealed; this was the first of the Ferrari road cars to feature this design. With an indent line running around the entire mid-section of the 365, the finish of the performance vehicle was also of a unique quality, with its upper half being the standard paint finish whilst the lower was finished in black satin paint; this eventually became

a styling that was employed on subsequent Ferrari models. While the 365 was constructed around the usual tubular steel-framed chassis with cross bracing, steel panels were used in the integral design of the forward cockpit section, creating a rigid and sturdy central cell. With only 387 of the 365 GT4 Berlinetta Boxer being manufactured during its three-year production period, this model above its subsequent siblings (the BB 512 in 1976 and the BB 512i in 1981) is the rarest of the series.

Produced	1973-1984
Engine Size	4390 cc
Cylinders	12
0-60 mph	5.4 secs
Top Speed	186 mph
Power Output	360 bhp
Transmission	Manual
Gears	5 Speed
Length	171.6 in (4360 mm)
Width	70.9 in (1800 mm)
Height	44.1 in (1120 mm)
Weight	2557 lb (1160 kg)
Wheelbase	98.4 in (2500 mm)

(Specifications refer to the Berlinetta Boxer 365 GT4)

ZV 60226

GT4

Unleashed at the Paris Motor Show in 1973, the 308 GT4 was a groundbreaking model for Ferrari. This angular 2+2 was the first Ferrari production car to feature Bertone bodywork, instead of the usual Pininfarina design, and critics compared its appearance to the Bertone-designed Lancia Stratos

Produced	1974-1980
Engine Size	2927 cc
Cylinders	8
0-60 mph	7.7 secs
Top Speed	156 mph
Power Output	250 bhp
Transmission	Manual
Gears	5 Speed
Length	169.3 in (4300 mm)
Width	70.9 in (1800 mm)
Height	46.5 in (1180 mm)
Weight	2701 lb (1255 kg)
Wheelbase	100.4 in (2550 mm)

(Specifications refer to the 308 GT4)

and the Lamborghini Urraco. The GT4 was also the first production vehicle to feature a mid-engined V8 layout.

For the first three years of its production the 308 GT4 carried the Dino badge, as the intention was to market the car as a supplement to the two-seater 246 GT/GTS in the Dino range, a recognized marque in its own right. However, in 1976 the GT4 received the iconic prancing horse badge.

The chassis, although based on that of the Dino 246, was stretched for a 100.4 in (2550 mm) wheelbase to make additional room for rear seats.

The transversely mounted 3L V8 engine produced 250 bhp, although models built for the US market generated 230 bhp. Later models featured a single-distributor engine instead of the twin-distributor version seen in earlier cars, and fog lamps mounted behind the front grille replaced those that were mounted ahead of the front valance.

With an aim to take advantage of a reduced tax burden on vehicles with engines smaller than two liters, the 208 GT4 2+2 was unveiled at the 1975 Geneva Motor Show. The 1991 cc power plant produced 180 bhp and boasted a top speed of 137 mph; it went down in the record books as the smallest production V8 in car manufacturing history. Visually, the 208 GT4 was distinguishable from the 308 GT4 by the absence of fog lights and narrower wheels.

As the 1970s drew to a close so did production of the GT4, with 2,138 308s rolling off the assembly line as opposed to just 880 of its smaller counterpart. It is, however, one of the more affordable second-hand Ferraris in the 21st century, although, as with many old classics, running costs can be astronomical.

3088 DF

308

Designed by Leonardo Fioravanti at Pininfarina, the 308 GTB was introduced at both the London and Paris Motor Shows in 1975 as a replacement for the Dino 246. The two-seater merged the use of bold lines with sweeping curves and has become one of the most recognized and iconic Ferraris to date, despite being one of their lower-end ranges. It shared the same V8 that was used in the 308 GT4, transversely mid-mounted with a displacement of 2926 cc and coupled with an all synchromesh

Produced	1975-1985
Engine Size	2926 cc
Cylinders	8
0-60 mph	6.2 secs
Top Speed	155 mph
Power Output	255 bhp
Transmission	Manual
Gears	5 Speed
Length	116.5 in (4230 mm)
Width	67.7 in (1720 mm)
Height	44.1 in (1120 mm)
Weight	2403 lb (1090 kg)
Wheelbase	92.5 in (2350 mm)

(Specifications refer to the 308 base model)

five-speed transmission. Power output was 255 bhp for European market models while US market

examples generated 240 bhp due to emission control devices.

The bodies of early models (1975-77) built by Carrozzeria Scaglietti were entirely constructed of fiberglass, resulting in a lightweight vehicle – it was the first time Ferrari had used fiberglass as a body material for a production car. However, this changed in June 1977 when they switched to using steel. It was during this year that Ferrari also introduced the targa-topped 308 GTS, a car that became famous on the popular television series *Magnum P.I.*, starring Tom Selleck.

Around 12,000 Ferrari 308s were built during their production years with only 712 fiberglass versions.

400

The 400 GT made its public debut at the 1976 Paris Motor Show to replace the previously popular 365 GT4 2+2 model. It shared a structurally identical chassis to its predecessor but subtle changes differentiate the two cars: a small body-colored spoiler is present on the lower edge of the nose and the iconic cavallino rampante was removed from the radiator grille. The interior was made more sumptuous; the seat upholstery, stitch style, and pattern were also changed.

The 4.8L V12 was front mounted and able to generate 339 bhp, achieve 0-60mph in 7.1 seconds, and power on to just under 150 mph at a maximum.

The 400 was the first Ferrari to have the option of automatic transmission; the 400 GT used a five-speed all synchromesh

Produced	1976-1989
Engine Size	4823 cc
Cylinders	12
0-60 mph	7.1 secs
Top Speed	149.1 mph
Power Output	339 bhp
Transmission	Manual or automatic
Gears	5 Speed
Length	189.4 in (4810 mm)
Width	70.8 in (1798 mm)
Height	51.7 in (1314 mm)
Weight	3979 lb (1805 kg)
Wheelbase	106.3 in (2700 mm)

(Specifications refer to the 400 GT)

transmission, while the 400A used the Turbo-Hydromatic THM400 from General Motors. Of the 503 cars built, only 147 were manual and 355 were automatic, indicating the direction in which the market was heading.

In 1979, the carburetors were replaced with Bosch K-Jetronic fuel injection, resulting in the 400i. This car received further upgrades in 1983 including a new interior, a body-colored rear panel, and front fog/driving lamps exposed in the grille.

Mondial

Produced	1980-1993
Engine Size	2926 cc
Cylinders	8
0-60 mph	9.4 secs
Top Speed	142 mph
Power Output	214 bhp
Transmission	Manual
Gears	5 Speed
Length	180.3 in (4580 mm)
Width	70.5 in (1790 mm)
Height	49.2 in (1250 mm)
Weight	3188 lb (1446 kg)
Wheelbase	104.3 in (2650 mm)

(Specifications refer to the Mondial 8)

The Pininfarina-designed Mondial made its first appearance at the Geneva Motor Show in 1980 as a replacement for the 308 models. The celebrated 500 Mondial race car inspired the name of Ferrari's 2+2 coupe. Renowned coachbuilder Carrozzeria Scaglietti designed the steel body, which was assembled on a lightweight steel box-section space frame and, for the first time in Ferrari history, the entire engine, gearbox, and rear suspension were mounted on a detachable sub frame. The mid/rear-mounted Bosch K-Jetronic fuel injection V8 was originally used in the 1973 Dino 308 GT4.

Two years after its initial introduction, Ferrari launched their Mondial QV (Quattrovalvole), which featured a new four-valve head. In 1983 they released the desirable Mondial Cabriolet, which quickly became a popular model within the American market.

The 3.2 version was announced in 1985, offering a more powerful and flexible V8, resulting in an enhanced performance. The comfortable and spacious interior featured a more ergonomic design. Available in a coupe and cabriolet form, the Mondial 3.2 was able to push 270 bhp, thanks to the V8 having larger bore and stroke giving a displacement of 3184 cc.

In 1989 the Mondial evolved for the final time resulting in the Mondial T – the "T" suffix in reference to the transversely mounted gearbox. Improved weight distribution and handling resulted from the lower placement of the engine, a 3.4L V8 capable of punching out a top speed of 156 mph.

The Mondial was one of Ferrari's most successful ranges, with more than 6,000 cars built during its 13-year run.

288 GTO

The Ferrari GTO (Gran Turismo Omologato), also known unofficially as the 288 GTO, was unveiled at the Geneva Motor Show in 1984, igniting a wave of enthusiasm. With its powerful V8 engine and contemporary racing-inspired chassis and sub frame, the GTO was the closest thing to a racing car available on the market. The body was largely made of fiberglass and composites, making it very advanced for its time. Kevlar, Nomex, and aluminum were used for the engine compartment, creating a perfect combination for heat resistance while also being strong and light. The GTO shared visual similarities with the mid-engined 308 GTB, and although a V8 engine powered both cars the similarities ended there. The GTO's engine was mid-mounted longitudinally in the chassis in order to make room for the twin turbochargers and intercoolers, and could produce 400 bhp at 7000 rpm. Acceleration from 0-60 was achieved in five seconds or less and the GTO could power on to a maximum speed of 190 mph. The GTO was available in one color only – the famed rosso red.

Ferrari intended to build 200 cars, however they went on to produce a total of 272 in order to meet customer demand – all of which sold before production even began.

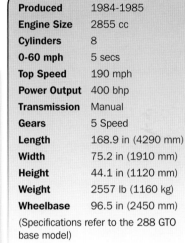

Produced	1984-1985
Engine Size	2855 cc
Cylinders	8
0-60 mph	5 secs
Top Speed	190 mph
Power Output	400 bhp
Transmission	Manual
Gears	5 Speed
Length	168.9 in (4290 mm)
Width	75.2 in (1910 mm)
Height	44.1 in (1120 mm)
Weight	2557 lb (1160 kg)
Wheelbase	96.5 in (2450 mm)

(Specifications refer to the 288 GTO base model)

Testarossa

In 1984 Ferrari introduced the Pininfarina-designed Testarossa at the Paris Motor Show. The name Testarossa translates from the Italian for "red head" – a name given to the car for the red-painted cam covers that it featured. Hailed for its 12-cylinder, 4.9L engine that reached a top speed of 180 mph and a 0-60 time of little more than five seconds, the Testarossa quickly became another of Ferrari's iconic production cars, with a retail price of $181,000 by 1989. As the successor to the Ferrari Berlinetta Boxer, the Testarossa featured many radical design changes, some of which had been the trademark styling of many Ferrari models for decades. No longer did the front end look sharp and boxy: a more rounded, soft approach had been explored. The striking and somewhat innovative design of the side air intakes gave the vehicle its iconic look; it was the twin side-mounted radiators that required the additional cooling provided by the tapering ventilation.

As a result of the Testarossa's mid-engine placement, which created a perfect gravitational balance between the front and rear axles, the car was boasted to feature a standing weight distribution of 40 per cent to the front and 60 per cent to the rear; inevitably this feature was destined to assist with better cornering and the general stability of the car on the road. A further radical design change in this sports car was that of the singular exterior mirror mounted on the driver's side of the vehicle. Whilst this was displeasing to some, it was not until 1987, during the Geneva Motor Show, that it was announced that

Produced	1984-1996
Engine Size	4943 cc
Cylinders	12
0-60 mph	5.2 secs
Top Speed	180 mph
Power Output	390 bhp
Transmission	Manual
Gears	5 Speed
Length	176.6 in (4485 mm)
Width	77.8 in (1976 mm)
Height	44.5 in (1130 mm)
Weight	3320 lb (1506 kg)
Wheelbase	100.4 in (2550 mm)

(Specifications refer to the Testarossa base model)

the design of the mirror had been changed to a more suitable position and matched by a passenger-side accompaniment.

In 1991 the standard Testarossa model was replaced by the 512 TR, which featured a better weight distribution (of 41 per cent to the front and 59 per cent to the rear), alongside larger intake valves, a better engine management system, and a broader power curve to assist with better acceleration. Later, in 1995, the industry also saw the introduction of the F512 M – it had better weight distribution than the 512 TR. By the time the cars were removed from the production line, Ferrari had manufactured close to 10,000 from the Testarossa, 512 TR, and F512 M line, making this series one of the most popular and widely sold Ferraris at the time.

328

The 328 GTB (Gran Turismo Berlinetta) was Ferrari's evolutionary upgrade of the 308 that preceded it. Fitted with a new 3.2L V8 and a smoother aerodynamic chassis, the Pininfarina design continued to impress critics and hold the attention of the public; the newly designed engine had an output of 85 bhp per liter, 3 bhp more than the 308 series before it. The 328 was first introduced to the motoring world at the 1985 Frankfurt Motor Show, alongside the Mondial 3.2 series. The car featured a smoother front end and tailpiece compared to the 308 and was hailed as one of Ferrari's easiest models to maintain, as most engine work could be carried out without lowering it from the chassis. The rear-engined 90° V8 punched out a top speed of 163 mph, with a power output of 270 bhp and was available with a five-speed manual transmission. The updated

Produced	1985-1989
Engine Size	3184 cc
Cylinders	8
0-60 mph	6.4 secs
Top Speed	163 mph
Power Output	270 bhp
Transmission	Manual
Gears	5 Speed
Length	167.5 in (4255 mm)
Width	68.1 in (1730 mm)
Height	44.4 in (1128 mm)
Weight	2784 lb (1263 kg)
Wheelbase	92.5 in (2350 mm)

(Specifications refer to the 328 GTB)

sporty physique provided a more aerodynamic styling and the 328 was recorded as having a 0-60 in 6.4 seconds, 0.2 seconds faster than the previous 308 design.

Built on a tubular chassis the 328 featured anti-roll bars all round, disc brakes with independent suspension (via wish bones), and hydraulic shock absorbers. Upon release, the 328 came with a variety of optional extras, including air conditioning, metallic paint, leather dashboard, and rear aerofoil (that appeared as standard on the Japanese models). In 1988 ABS was introduced as an option for the 328, however this meant that the suspension geometry and wheel design had to be redesigned in order to accommodate the modifications. The original list price of the 328 started from $58,400 in the US for the standard model. It wasn't until four years after the 328 – available as the GTB coupe or the GTS targa top – had been first introduced to the production line that Ferrari ceased its manufacture; the 328 was later replaced by the 348 TB in the fall of 1989.

F40

At the turn of Ferrari's 40th anniversary of being an active manufacturer in the automotive trade, the company produced the F40 as a token of their achievements. Designed once again by Pininfarina, the F40 two-seater coupe was the last ever Ferrari design to be personally approved by Enzo Ferrari before his unfortunate passing in 1988. The car took critics by surprise, with its racing car aesthetics, futuristic design, and the fact that it was 100 per cent road-legal. The car featured a five-speed manual transmission and body-length intake vents that assisted with cooling, alongside a wide rear window positioned just above the engine, framed by its boastful and iconic rear wing. The remarkably designed rear-engined

Produced	1987-1992
Engine Size	2936 cc
Cylinders	8
0-60 mph	3.8 secs
Top Speed	201 mph
Power Output	471 bhp
Transmission	Manual
Gears	5 Speed
Length	174.4 in (4430 mm)
Width	77.9 in (1980 mm)
Height	44.5 in (1130 mm)
Weight	2767 lb (1255 kg)
Wheelbase	96.5 in (2450 mm)

(Specifications refer to the F40 base model)

F40, with a top speed of 201 mph, yielded 471 bhp from a 90° V8 engine, with a 0-60 in around four seconds. Two years after its launch, in 1989 the F40 was one of the most sought-after vehicles during the "super car boom," with clients willing to pay more than double the suggested retail price in order to get their hands on one. Ferrari left the production period of the F40 open-ended due to its popularity, but finally halted the production line in 1992 after 1,315 vehicles had been manufactured.

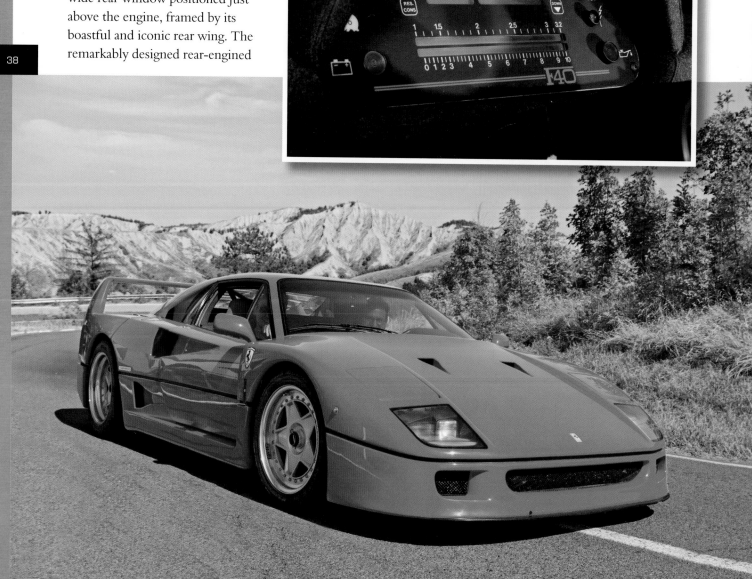

348

In 1989, Ferrari unveiled the 348 TB and TS (convertible) models at the Frankfurt Motor Show: the first completely new design since the passing of Enzo Ferrari in August 1988. With a brand new transverse gearbox and evident bodywork modifications, the 348 was designed to make a statement. The Ferrari 348 TB (the "T" standing for transverse, whilst the "B" was the Berlinetta coupe styling) was a radically redesigned version of its predecessor, the 328: most notably, the redesigned flanks that featured intakes reminiscent of the Testarossa and the remolded front end of the vehicle that gave it a prestigious

Produced	1989-1995
Engine Size	3405 cc
Cylinders	8
0-60 mph	6 secs
Top Speed	171 mph
Power Output	300 bhp
Transmission	Manual
Gears	5 Speed
Length	166.5 in (4230 mm)
Width	74.6 in (1894 mm)
Height	46.1 in (1170 mm)
Weight	2767 lb (1255 kg)
Wheelbase	96.5 in (2450 mm)

(Specifications refer to the 348 base model)

new look. With a longitudinally 90°-mounted V8 engine that packed an impressive 300 bhp, it's no wonder the manufacturers boasted of the high torsional strength of

238 lb/ft that was translated straight to the road. With an impressive 0-60 in six seconds and a top speed of 171 mph, the 348 was evidently a faster vehicle than its predecessor.

Other features of the 348 design were the dual-computerized engine management system, self-diagnosing air conditioning and heating systems, and anti-lock brakes. The coolant radiators were moved from the nose end to the rear sides, allowing for the tapered Testarossa-style intakes to be included. The 348 was fitted with electric windows and mirrors as standard in the early stages of production; the inclusion of heating elements that were activated by the rear windows demister switch was later added.

456

Designed by Lorenzo Ramaciotti at Pininfarina, the 456 grand tourer was first publicly on show during October 1992 where it debuted in Paris. At the time of production the 456 was dubbed as one of the fastest production four-seaters, as it

Produced	1992-2003
Engine Size	5473 cc
Cylinders	12
0-60 mph	5.2 secs
Top Speed	188 mph
Power Output	436 bhp
Transmission	Manual
Gears	6 Speed
Length	186.2 in (4730 mm)
Width	75.6 in (1920 mm)
Height	51.2 in (1300 mm)
Weight	3726 lb (1690 kg)
Wheelbase	102.4 in (2600 mm)

(Specifications refer to the 456 base model)

could push 188 mph while carrying four passengers. Boasting 436 bhp coupled with an impressive 0-60 in 5.2 seconds, it was no wonder that the 456 put Ferrari back on the map with this 65° V12 front-engined model. While elements of the chassis design were evidently inspired by the Daytona, the 456 featured a sleek new body curvature and was the last ever Ferrari model to feature the signature retractable headlights. Manufactured using the common steel tube frame, the 456 was covered largely with aluminum panels, specially welded to the steel using a sandwich material called Feran: a specially formulated composite material that allowed the two distinctively different metals to be welded. The 456 later underwent some improvements with regard to its aerodynamic design and some engine cooling upgrades when the 456 M was released in 1998.

F355

The stunning Pininfarina-designed F355 is a rear-wheel driven sports car with a 3496 cc, 90°-mounted V8 that kicks out an exceptional 380 bhp. This new Ferrari was an engineering masterpiece of its time, both visually and in terms of performance. The F355 was first unveiled at the 1994 Geneva Motor Show, with its unique five-valve cylinder head that produced impressive torque and better intake permeability, resulting in a much faster road vehicle. With its unique shape and aerodynamic design, the F355 undertook over 1,300 hours of wind tunnel testing before the final body shaping was agreed. The entire aerodynamic design of the car was built and honed around the underbody: a full-body under tray that was built with the intention of matching the downforce of the front and rear axles. With Pirelli tires, power steering, anti-roll bars, and two switchable driving modes ("sport" and "comfort") as standard, the original launch price of $130,000 was deemed as exceptional value. Aside from the Berlinetta coupe, Ferrari also released the F355 as a targa top GTS at launch, and later in 1995 the Spider convertible model.

Produced	1994-1999
Engine Size	3496 cc
Cylinders	8
0-60 mph	4.9 secs
Top Speed	183 mph
Power Output	380 bhp
Transmission	Manual
Gears	6 Speed
Length	167.3 in (4250 mm)
Width	74.8 in (1900 mm)
Height	46.1 in (1170 mm)
Weight	2976 lb (1350 kg)
Wheelbase	96.5 in (2450 mm)

(Specifications refer to the F355 base model)

F50

The F50 was the first car to take Formula 1 technology and utilize it in a production vehicle. Unveiled during the 1995 Geneva Motor Show, the Pininfarina-designed Ferrari F50 was the celebratory design model of the company's 50th anniversary. The F50 was stripped of many of the mod-cons that most would expect, such as power steering, ABS, and power assisted braking, however these were replaced by the purist aerodynamic design, a 4.7L engine, and F1-inspired body shape that made the F50 what it is. With only 349 of these exquisite vehicles having been produced in its two-year production period, it was no wonder that the retail price ranged from $480,000-$555,000. The F50 features a 65° V12 that boasts an egotistical design drafted in from F1 models, enabling an impressive top speed of 202 mph that punches out 513 bhp and 0-60

Produced	1995-1997
Engine Size	4700 cc
Cylinders	12
0-60 mph	3.7 secs
Top Speed	202 mph
Power Output	513 bhp
Transmission	Manual
Gears	6 Speed
Length	176.4 in (4480 mm)
Width	78.2 in (1986 mm)
Height	43.9 in (1116 mm)
Weight	2910 lb (1320 kg)
Wheelbase	101.6 in (2580 mm)

(Specifications refer to the F50 base model)

in just 3.7 seconds. It is the derived composite body materials and design that truly gave the car its F1 qualities; a monocoque chassis was best suited for the various intakes, exhaust slots, and aerodynamic curves, while the more elaborate rear wing was a suggestive advance in design from its predecessor, the F40. All 349 examples of the F50 feature a removable hard top and, boldly, Ferrari offered the car in five different colors: two different shades of red, yellow, black, and silver.

42

550

First introduced at the Nürburgring in 1996, the Pininfarina-designed front-engined 550 was Ferrari's answer to a powerful V12 coupe, with a top speed of 200 mph, utilizing 480 bhp. With a 5.5L engine and six-speed manual gearbox, this new aerodynamic design was built as a high-performance production vehicle. The 550 Maranello obtained critical acclaim when it established new records for a production car during speed tests carried out in Marysville, Ohio, in October 1998, when it was recorded as having an average speed of 188.88 mph over a distance of 62 miles. The construction of the rear-wheel driven 550 boasted a steel tubular frame with aluminum panels that were bolted on in order to support its sturdiness and rugged visual aesthetic. In 2000 the Barchetta design was unleashed at the Paris Motor Show. The Barchetta, simply being the convertible option of the 550, was manufactured without a hard top, but with a soft top that was issued with an advisory caution that it should not be used above speeds of 70 mph. The 550 was a faster and more practical sports car than its predecessor, the F512 M.

Produced	1996-2001
Engine Size	5474 cc
Cylinders	12
0-60 mph	4.6 secs
Top Speed	200 mph
Power Output	480 bhp
Transmission	Manual
Gears	6 Speed
Length	179.3 in (4554 mm)
Width	76.2 in (1935 mm)
Height	50.3 in (1278 mm)
Weight	3730 lb (1692 kg)
Wheelbase	98.4 in (2500 mm)

(Specifications refer to the 550 base model)

360

The Ferrari 360 was a two-seater, mid-engined, rear-wheel drive coupe produced between 1999 and 2005. Unveiled at the Geneva Motor Show in 1999, the 360 replaced the F355 range that had enjoyed five years in production with no additional cosmetic changes. Ferrari partnered with Alcoa to develop a new aluminum space-frame chassis that weighed 28 per cent lighter while being 40 per cent stiffer than the frame of the F355; the result was Ferrari's first car to be entirely constructed in aluminum. Designed by Pininfarina, the styling deviated from the sharp angles and retractable headlamps that were often seen in previous Ferraris. Instead, the design adopted smooth curvature and aerodynamic

Produced	1999-2005
Engine Size	3586 cc
Cylinders	8
0-60 mph	4.3 secs
Top Speed	189 mph
Power Output	400 bhp
Transmission	Manual
Gears	6 Speed
Length	176.3 in (4478 mm)
Width	75.7 in (1923 mm)
Height	47.8 in (1214 mm)
Weight	3064 lb (1390 kg)
Wheelbase	102.4 in (2600 mm)

(Specifications refer to the 360 base model)

considerations, including the front-featured twin radiator inlet grilles that played an active role in the increased downforce as the car's speed rose. The 360 was the first Ferrari to use a clear glass engine cover, enabling enthusiasts to see the masterpiece in full view.

The new V8 generated 400 bhp, and the combination of a lighter car and more powerful engine resulted in improved acceleration performance compared to the F355. The 360 sprinted from 0-60 in 4.3 seconds and could achieve a top speed of 189 mph.

The 360 Modena was the first model in production, the name deriving from the birthplace of Enzo Ferrari. Vehicles were available with a six-speed manual

or F1 electrohydraulic manual transmission. Two years after the launch of the Modena, Ferrari announced its 20th road-going convertible – the 360 Spider. Similar to the Modena, the Spider featured the mid-mounted 400 bhp V8 engine that was visible under a glass cover, and the engineers at Ferrari cleverly designed the roof to automatically fold away into its own compartment between the cabin and the engine bay.

The final model, the Challenge Stradale, was a special edition high-performance road-legal version of the 360 Modena that made its debut at the Geneva Motor Show in 2003. Experience in the International Ferrari Trofeo Pirelli Challenge and GT competitions

enabled engineers to modify the Challenge Stradale into something completely unique. Reducing the weight by 242 lb (110 kg) and major modifications to the V8 engine boosted performance. While aluminum remained the

main construction material for the chassis and body, carbon fiber was introduced for structural elements. The aerodynamic styling was honed and a lower racing setup increased downforce by 50 per cent in comparison to the Modena.

575M Maranello

The 575M Maranello was a two-seater grand tourer launched in 2002 as an updated and improved version of its 550 predecessor. The 575 indicated the displacement had been enhanced from 5500 cc to 5750 cc, which resulted in increased power and torque, while the "M" suffix stood for "modificato" (modified). In addition to the larger engine, mechanical improvements included an altered weight distribution, refined aerodynamics, adaptive suspension, and the Magneti Marelli paddle-shift

Produced	2002-2006
Engine Size	5750 cc
Cylinders	12
0-60 mph	4.1 secs
Top Speed	202 mph
Power Output	514 bhp
Transmission	Manual and "F1" electrohydraulic
Gears	6 Speed
Length	179.1 in (4550 mm)
Width	76.2 in (1935 mm)
Height	50.3 in (1277 mm)
Weight	2834 lb (1739 kg)
Wheelbase	98.4 in (2500 mm)

(Specifications refer to the 575M Maranello base model)

Formula 1 transmission – used for the first time in a 12-cylinder Ferrari road car.

The 575M had optimum weight distribution with a 50-50 split between the axles due to the transaxle design with a combined rear-mounted gearbox and differential unit. Locating the transmission in-between the rear wheels reduced shift times for the electrohydraulic gear selector.

Designed by Lorenzo Ramaciotti at Pininfarina, the idea was to adapt the look of the 550 through

minor styling, capturing a sober and balanced appearance in order to create the look of an instant classic, perfectly complementing Ferrari's return to a front-engined high-performance road car.

Three years after its official launch Ferrari announced their GTC handling package for the 575M Maranello. Designed to enhance the performance of the vehicle the kit included carbo-ceramic brake discs, racing brake pads, lower and more rigid vehicle setup, and unique 19-inch multi-piece wheel rims.

In 2005 Ferrari introduced the 575M Superamerica as a convertible version of the 575M Maranello. Featuring an electrochromic glass panel roof that rotated 180° to lie flat over the boot, this intelligent roof mechanism was previously used on a Leonardo Fioravanti-designed Alfa Romeo Vola concept car.

The Superamerica boasted a power output of 533 bhp and was marketed as the world's fastest convertible Berlinetta, topping speeds of 199 mph. Enzo Ferrari maintained that there should always be one car fewer available than what the market was demanding and the 575M Superamerica was no exception; as a limited edition model only 599 cars were built.

Enzo (F60)

Race-derived technology has always been applied to Ferrari production cars, and the limited edition run of F60s celebrated the company's Formula 1 prowess and marked the start of a new generation of V12 engines. The completely new rear-mounted 65° V12 delivered intense power and massive torque at low revs; with a displacement of 5998 cc the engine punched out a maximum power output of 660 bhp at 7800 rpm. Extensive wind tunnel and track testing influenced the streamlined shape, and a carbon fiber body, ceramic composite disc brakes, and F1-style electrohydraulic shift transmission demonstrated the Formula 1 technology applied. The six-speed electrohydraulic system automatically disengaged the clutch, activated a gear change, and ordered a burst of torque from the engine in just 150 ms. The F60 also featured traction control and active aerodynamics to generate exceptional downforce. In terms of performance the Enzo could accelerate from 0-60 in a mere 3.4 seconds and reach an impressive 217 mph flat out.

The 60th anniversary model was named Ferrari Enzo in honor of the founder, who believed that the design of production cars should be influenced by racers. A limited run of just 399 cars was built and only those who Ferrari deemed worthy of their new creation were invited to purchase one. Buyers were invited to the factory so that their new car could receive a tailor-made cockpit that reflected their individual needs, including positioning of the accelerator and brake pedals. In 2004 Ferrari produced a 400th car, specially built to be auctioned for charity by the Vatican. Auctioned by Sotheby's the top-of-the-range Enzo fetched $1.1 million – double the original retail price.

Produced	2002-2004
Engine Size	5998 cc
Cylinders	12
0-60 mph	3.4 secs
Top Speed	217 mph
Power Output	660 bhp
Transmission	Semi-automatic
Gears	6 Speed
Length	185.1 in (4702 mm)
Width	80.1 in (2035 mm)
Height	45.2 in (1147 mm)
Weight	3020 lb (1370 kg)
Wheelbase	104.3 in (2650 mm)

(Specifications refer to the Enzo [F60] base model)

The Enzo has also been used as the starting point for other vehicles, such as the Ferrari FXX and P4/5 as well as the Maserati MC12 (Ferrari owned a 50 per cent share in the company between 1997 and 2005).

Enzo Ferrari   Maranello, 25 giugno 2002

612 Scaglietti

Produced	2004-2011
Engine Size	5748 cc
Cylinders	12
0-60 mph	4 secs
Top Speed	199 mph
Power Output	540 bhp
Transmission	Manual and sequential
Gears	6 Speed
Length	193 in (4902 mm)
Width	77 in (1957 mm)
Height	52.9 in (1344 mm)
Weight	4059 lb (1840 kg)
Wheelbase	116.1 in (2950 mm)

(Specifications refer to the 612 Scaglietti base model)

Designed by Pininfarina and named in honor of the legendary Sergio Scaglietti responsible for the styling of some of Ferrari's most beautiful cars of the 1950s and 1960s, the 612 Scaglietti offered the perfect fusion of innovation and design with unprecedented comfort. Since the launch of the 1948 166 Inter, Ferrari has produced a number of successful 2+2s, with each generation pushing the boundaries of technology and sophistication, and the 612 Scaglietti was no exception. The dynamic mid-front-mounted V12 engine had been situated further back and active suspension allowed the car to automatically adapt to road conditions. Generating a magnificent 540 bhp, the 612 could achieve 0-60 in four seconds and power on to 199 mph. In addition to manual transmission, the Scaglietti was available with a F1A electrohydraulic gearbox, reducing gear-shift times by 100 ms in high-performance driving situations.

The aluminum chassis and bodywork were remarkably light, offering enhanced benefits to performance, comfort, and handling. The Scaglietti's most notable feature was the panoramic electrochromic roof extending from windscreen to rear window with three tint settings giving the illusion of driving an open top car.

F430

The F430 made its official debut at the Paris Motor Show in 2004, indicating a brand new generation of Ferrari eight-cylinder models, demonstrating exceptional engineering and Formula 1 influence. The F430 boasted two innovations for production cars – the electronic differential (E-Diff) and the commutator switch (better known as the manettino by Ferrari racing drivers) on the steering wheel that allows the driver to

Produced	2004-2009
Engine Size	4308 cc
Cylinders	8
0-60 mph	4.4 secs
Top Speed	196 mph
Power Output	483 bhp
Transmission	Manual and F1 electrohydraulic manual
Gears	6 Speed
Length	177.6 in (4511 mm)
Width	75.7 in (1923 mm)
Height	47.8 in (1214 mm) Coupe or 48.6 in (1234 mm) Spider
Weight	3197 lb (1450 kg)
Wheelbase	102.4 in (2600 mm)

(Specifications refer to the F430 base model)

experience quick and simple adjustments to suspension, traction control, E-Diff, and the change speed of the F1 transmission. The settings available included sport, race, ice, and low grip conditions. The electronic differential, initially developed for Ferrari F1 single-seaters, transferred huge torque levels while offering maximum grip coming out of bends.

In terms of styling, the F430 shared the basic Alcoa aluminum chassis, roof line, doors, and glass that were used for the 360, however, revision to the aerodynamic design resulted in improved efficiency with downforce greatly increased. The 4.3L engine marked the departure of the previously used Dino racing program V8 descendants. Powered by a new 90° V8, derived from a shared Ferrari/Maserati design, the F430 could accelerate from 0-60 in 4.4 seconds and punched out a maximum speed of 196 mph.

599

Named after its 5999 cc displacement, Gran Turismo Berlinetta nature, and the Fiorano Circuit test track, the 599 GTB Fiorano was unveiled at the 2006 Geneva Motor Show as Ferrari's most powerful V12-engined production car to date. It certainly met expectations, demonstrating its 0-60 sprint in 3.7 seconds and powering on to a top speed of

Produced	2006-2012
Engine Size	5999 cc
Cylinders	12
0-60 mph	3.7 secs
Top Speed	205 mph
Power Output	612 bhp
Transmission	Manual and automated manual
Gears	6 Speed
Length	183.7 in (4665 mm)
Width	77.2 in (1962 mm)
Height	52.6 in (1336 mm)
Weight	3721 lb (1688 kg)
Wheelbase	108.3 in (2750 mm)

(Specifications refer to the 599 base model)

205 mph. Designed by Pininfarina, the objective was to retain the Ferrari trademark of sportiness while exploring innovative lines, with each surface perfectly sculpted to incorporate aerodynamic technology. Extensive testing in the wind tunnel and optimization of the car's flat underbody led to superior results in terms of downforce and drag reduction.

The 65° V12 engine was built using the same basic design as the Enzo engine, and further developments allowed for high engine revs and reduced weight. Mounted in a mid-front position, the engine delivered smooth power delivery and enhanced performance. This, coupled with an F1-superfast gearbox, bolstered the car's unique strength.

The powerful 599 GTB Fiorano was another symbolic sports car in Ferrari production history, joining the myriad of 12-cylinder two-seaters that proudly bear the prancing horse badge.

California

Produced	2008-present
Engine Size	4297 cc
Cylinders	8
0-60 mph	3.9 secs
Top Speed	193 mph
Power Output	453 bhp
Transmission	Dual-clutch automated manual
Gears	7 Speed
Length	179.6 in (4563 mm)
Width	74.9 in (1902 mm)
Height	51.5 in (1308 mm)
Weight	3593 lb (1630 kg)
Wheelbase	105.1 in (2670 mm)

(Specifications refer to the California base model)

Reviving the "California" name used for the 1950s Ferrari 250 GT, the 21st-century Ferrari California offers a compact, sporty appearance to its 2+2 hardtop convertible styling. The new California employs a number of innovations for Ferrari: it was the first car to use a seven-speed dual-clutch transmission, multi-link rear suspension, and to be powered by a front mid-mounted gasoline injection V8 engine. More than 1,000 hours were spent on perfecting its aerodynamics. The California can accelerate from 0-60 in 3.9 seconds and push on to a maximum speed of 193 mph. The inclusion of an optimized traction control system, originally introduced on the 599 GTB Fiorano, allows less experienced drivers to release the car's performance potential. The F1-Trac offers faster and more precise stability, resulting in an increase of 20 per cent in acceleration on exiting curves.

In 2012 Ferrari announced an upgraded California, which weighed 66.1 lb (30 kg) less than its 2009 counterpart in order to enhance performance ability. In 2014 the California T was unveiled at the Geneva Motor Show. The eagerly anticipated upgrade boasts an eight-cylinder turbo engine to deliver high performance while also featuring the most recently evolved F1-Trac traction control unit to maximize acceleration out of corners.

458

Although the 458 is described by Ferrari as the successor to the F430, it encompassed an entirely new design in terms of engine, aerodynamics, and styling. The 90° V8 mid-rear-mounted engine is designed to produce 562 bhp at 9000 rpm – a first for a road car with the eight-cylinder capacity. The seven-speed dual-clutch transmission from Getrag guarantees faster and smoother changes and is able to change gear in 0.04 seconds. Maximum torque is 540 Nm at 6000 rpm with 80 per cent torque available at 3250 rpm.

Pininfarina's design approach integrates simplicity and lightness while incorporating the heavily influenced requirement for aerodynamic technology. A single opening in the front grille and aerodynamic profiling directs air to the coolant radiators. Downforce is generated by small aeroelastic winglets that deform at high speeds, reducing drag. Former Ferrari F1 racing driver Michael Schumacher played an important role in the interior design of the 458; similar to racing cars, many of the controls and features are situated on the steering wheel as opposed to on the dashboard.

Produced	2010-present
Engine Size	4499 cc
Cylinders	8
0-60 mph	3.3 secs
Top Speed	201.8 mph
Power Output	562 bhp
Transmission	Dual-clutch Getrag
Gears	7 Speed
Length	178.2 in (4527 mm)
Width	76.3 in (1937 mm)
Height	47.8 in (1213 mm)
Weight	3302 lb (1498 kg)
Wheelbase	104.3 in (2650 mm)

(Specifications refer to the 458 base model)

FF

The Ferrari Four, simply known by its acronym FF, was introduced at the 2011 Geneva Motor Show. Replacing the 612 Scaglietti grand tourer, the FF arrived on the scene as a revolutionary four-seater and with Ferrari's first ever four-wheel drive system. The FF exudes sophistication and versatility, thanks to Pininfarina's perfectly proportioned design combined with the exceptional performance ability created by the 65° V12 direct injection engine. Achieving

Produced	2011-present
Engine Size	6262 cc
Cylinders	12
0-60 mph	3.7 secs
Top Speed	208 mph
Power Output	660 bhp
Transmission	Dual-clutch automated semi-automatic
Gears	7 Speed
Length	193.1 in (4907 mm)
Width	76.9 in (1953 mm)
Height	54.3 in (1379 mm)
Weight	4145 lb (1880 kg)
Wheelbase	117.7 in (2990 mm)

(Specifications refer to the FF base model)

0-60 in a mere 3.7 seconds, and with a top speed of 208 mph, it may come as a surprise that the FF offers practicality as well as power. It can comfortably accommodate four people and still offer 450L of boot space, while the four-wheel drive technology means that the FF can be used on low grip or snow-covered roads, as well as the track.

The interior offers luxurious comfort; customers can select a number of personalization options including specially selected aniline leather for the interior trim. Such luxury does come at a price, however, with the FF costing $300,000.

F12berlinetta

Unveiled at the 2012 Geneva Motor Show, the F12berlinetta replaces the 599 series and offers an improved specification of the 599 GTB Fiorano. The 65° V12 is more powerful and efficient, producing 750 bhp and enabling a top speed of 211 mph. Fuel efficiency has been improved with this car too, in fact it is 30 per cent more efficient than the 599, and Ferrari's HELE stop-start system reduces fuel consumption when idle.

The space-frame chassis was co-produced with Scaglietti, utilizing 12 different aluminum alloys to improve structural rigidity while also reducing weight. Inspired by F1 design, the F12berlinetta employs aerodynamic technology, developed with wind tunnel testing and extensive computational fluid dynamics simulations (CFD). Downforce is created by the Aero Bridge, an air channel that runs from the bonnet along each side of the car, which also gives the F12berlinetta a notable feature. Aerodynamic drag is reduced by the Active Brake Cooling ducts, which only open when the brakes are hot.

On the Fiorano test circuit it was able to achieve a lap in one minute 23 seconds – one second faster than the 599 GTO.

Produced	2012-present
Engine Size	6262 cc
Cylinders	12
0-60 mph	3.1 secs
Top Speed	211 mph
Power Output	750 bhp
Transmission	Dual-clutch automated manual
Gears	7 Speed
Length	181.8 in (4618 mm)
Width	76.4 in (1942 mm)
Height	50.1 in (1273 mm)
Weight	3594 lb (1630 kg)
Wheelbase	107.1 in (2720 mm)

(Specifications refer to the F12berlinetta base model)

LaFerrari (aka F70 or F150)

Also known as the F70, the LaFerrari is the first mild hybrid (typically mainly powered by an internal combustion engine alongside an electric motor that enables the engine to be negated when stopped, braking, or coasting) produced by Ferrari to mark the 70th anniversary of motoring success. The eagerly awaited limited production sports car was unveiled at the 2013 Geneva Motor Show and is the first car since the 1973 Bertone-styled Dino 308 GT4 not to receive Pininfarina bodywork or styling. While boasting the highest power output of any Ferrari, the innovative technology has allowed fuel consumption to be cut by 40 per cent.

A team led by Flavio Manzoni have perfectly balanced and emphasized both beauty and ability in their design of LaFerrari. Inspired by F1 models, the carbon fiber body has been aerodynamically sculpted into an innovative design and the low bonnet accentuates the muscular wheel arches. Fernando Alonso and Felipe Massa both played an active part in the car's development, which has a similar driving position to a single-seater F1 car.

Powered by the mid-rear-mounted 65° V12 and supplemented by the HY-KERS (kinetic energy reduction system) unit, LaFerrari promises top-level performance in both power and speed, delivering 950 bhp and 0-60 in less than three seconds. Punching out a top speed of 217 mph, LaFerrari has recorded a lap time of just 1 minute 30 seconds on the Fiorano Test Circuit.

Produced	2013-present
Engine Size	6262 cc
Cylinders	12
0-60 mph	< 3 secs
Top Speed	217 mph
Power Output	950 bhp
Transmission	Dual-clutch automated manual
Gears	7 Speed
Length	185.1 in (4702 mm)
Width	78.4 in (1992 mm)
Height	43.9 in (1116 mm)
Weight	2767 lb (1255 kg)
Wheelbase	104.3 in (2650 mm)

(Specifications refer to the LaFerrari base model)

Ferrari's Sporting Pedigree

Ferrari have enjoyed more than six decades of Formula 1 success since the inaugural season in 1950. Their success in Formula 1 to date has been unrivaled and the team can boast a number of significant records including: most wins (season and all time), most fastest laps, most Grands Prix participated, and most pole positions, to name but a few.

Scuderia Ferrari is the longest-standing team in Grand Prix racing and statistically they are the most successful, boasting 15 World Drivers' Championship titles, 16 World Constructors' Championship titles, and 221 Grand Prix victories. The majority of Scuderia Ferrari's success arose from Formula 1 but

■ **ABOVE: At the British Grand Prix in 2001, Michael Schumacher drove two laps in the Ferrari 375 that Froilán González had driven at Silverstone in 1951 to claim Ferrari's first F1 victory.**

the team has successfully competed in various levels of motorsport since their formation in 1929.

The Formula 1 World Championship was established in 1950 and the team made their racing debut with a supercharged 1.5L V12-engined 125 F1 at the Monaco Grand Prix after missing the first race of the championship due to a dispute over the start money paid to entrants. The Alfa Romeo team dominated the first season in 1950, but Ferrari broke their winning streak when José Froilán González achieved the team's first victory in 1951 in the British Grand Prix. The following year Ferrari entered their 2L four-cylinder Tipo 500 and went on to win almost every race

for which it was entered. However, the success was short lived and subsequent seasons were turbulent due to changes in rules for 2.5L engines and disputes among team members.

In 1961 they won the first of their 16 Constructors' Championship titles, with Phil Hill leading the team, and followed this with the 1964 Championship, however, they would have to wait until 1975 to win the title again. Scuderia Ferrari's departure from world sports car racing two years previous enabled them to

■ ABOVE: American Phil Hill, garlanded after his victory in the 32nd Italian Grand Prix, waves to admirers at the Monza circuit in September 1961.

focus their efforts on Formula 1 and the sacrifice paid off: for the next two years they retained the Constructors' Championship. In fact, between 1975 and 1983 Ferrari secured six Constructors' crowns before a barren spell was ended with the arrival of Michael Schumacher in 1999. The 1976 season has been immortalized on the silver screen as the rivalry between Ferrari's Niki Lauda and McLaren's James Hunt erupted both on and off the track in Ron Howard's 2013 movie, *Rush*. As well as running their own team, Ferrari have regularly supplied

■ ABOVE: Michael Schumacher celebrates his win in the Canadian Grand Prix at the Circuit Gilles Villeneuve in Montreal, June 2004. Schumacher and Rubens Barrichello went on to finish first and second in the 2004 World Drivers' Championship.

■ RIGHT: Fernando Alonso at the FIA Formula 1 World Championship, Australian Grand Prix, March 2014.

engines for other teams, including Sauber, Red Bull, and Force India.

Over the years the Scuderia Ferrari team has included some of the world's most renowned drivers such as Phil Hill, Niki Lauda, Juan Manuel Fangio, and seven-times World Champion Michael Schumacher. Schumacher and Rubens Barrichello consolidated Ferrari's dominance on the track in 2004, when they finished first and second respectively in the World Drivers' Championship. Ferrari also dominated the Constructors' Championship: Schumacher won first place in 13 of 18 races, and 12 of the first 13 in the season (his only non-finish following a collision with Juan Pablo Montoya in Monaco), which were both Formula 1 records. Two more Constructors' titles followed in 2007 and 2008, before

the dominance of Red Bull and Sebastian Vettel.

The drivers for the 2014 season are Fernando Alonso, for the fourth year running, and 2007 World Champion Kimi Räikkönen. Team Principal Jean Todt was replaced in 2007 by Stefano Domenicali who resigned in April 2014. Marco Mattiacci was appointed soon after.

Scuderia Ferrari have also competed in Formula 2 and sports car racing from the late 1940s until the 1970s. They won the World Sportscar Championships 13 times and were a dominant force in the sector, winning 24 Hours of Le Mans for six consecutive years. They departed from sports car racing in 1973 to focus their efforts solely on Formula 1. However, Ferrari cars continued on in GT racing by other entrants aside from the Scuderia team.

Concept Cars and the Future

Ferrari have always been one of the world's leading prestige manufacturers, with revolutionary and innovative ideas. For every success on the track came a wave of innovation to be applied to their production cars. The F1 gearbox is one of the most important technological transfers from racing car to grand tourer. It was first tested in the Type 639 prototype before use in the Grand Prix Ferrari F1-89 that won the first race of the 1989 season when Nigel Mansell scored an unexpected victory in Brazil. Steering wheel mounted controls allowed the driver to change gear without the use of a clutch pedal and the success of such a feat caused Ferrari to consider its application in road-going vehicles. In 1992, 100 examples of the Mondial T experienced the potential of automatic transmission with acceleration times reduced. Over the subsequent years the F1 gearbox has received numerous improvements, benefiting both racing and road-going models. Formula 1 traction control was first introduced to road-going cars with the 599 GTB Fiorano model in 2006. Known as F1-Trac, a dedicated team transferred the relevant technology for a production vehicle to enable improved acceleration out of corners, and refined control of drive wheel-spin.

A composite chassis using

■ **BELOW:** Winner Nigel Mansell in his Ferrari at the Brazilian Grand Prix, Rio de Janeiro, March 1989.

four different types of carbon fiber deriving directly from F1 technology has also been applied to production cars. Despite the extra weight required for housing hybrid components, the overall chassis is 20 per cent lighter in comparison to that of the F60 Enzo Ferrari.

Ferrari have always been at the forefront of innovative design and technology and throughout the years have produced dozens of concept cars. In 2008, a version of the F430 Spider that runs on ethanol was on display at the Detroit Motor Show. Named the F430 Spider Bio Fuel, it shares the same 4.3L V8 engine capable of generating 500 bhp, with a four per cent increase and torque and five per cent less carbon dioxide emissions than its standard counterpart. The prototype was never on the agenda for mass

■ ABOVE: The Ferrari 599 HY-KERS at the 2010 Geneva Motor Show.

production as an alternative fuel solution, but represents one step toward the future. Their aim was to reduce CO_2 emissions by 40 per cent by 2012 through weight reduction and direct injection. Two years on and Ferrari unveiled their 599 HY-KERS vettura laboratorio at the 2010 Geneva Motor Show to illustrate how the latest hybrid technology could provide one possible solution for future models… irrespective of if they are V8 or V12 powered. Formula 1 engineering had provided the approach to hybrid technology used in production cars that doesn't negatively affect performance. An electric motor attached to the rear of the F1 dual clutch gearbox provides an instantaneous burst of torque when moving away from a standstill and during overtaking maneuvers. In slow city driving the hybrid system can fully function as a full-electric drivetrain. The overall result is that its power is coupled between the electric motor and the 6L V12. The electric unit also acts as a generator under braking, using kinetic energy to recharge the batteries. The 599 HY-KERS was reported to reduce CO_2 emissions by 35 per cent.

The next generation of Ferraris is set to be turbocharged, as strict consumption and emission regulations will affect the future of engineering. Ferrari chairman Luca di Montezemolo has stated that they will be making fewer cars than the market demands in order to maintain the exclusivity of their brand. The agenda includes more special editions, tailor-made varieties, and one-off models, although their core business will still lie in the GT road car market.

■ ABOVE: Ferrari CEO Luca di Montezemolo speaks during the press day at the 84th Geneva International Motor Show in Geneva, Switzerland, March 2014.